IMPROVISE BY LEARNING HOW T(
—a workbook in jazz improvisation for piano and all other m

(Intermediate Level)
by LEE EVANS

INTRODUCTION

This book introduces the student to basic improvisational and compositional techniques, mainly through the use of blues structure. Particular emphasis is given to techniques of melodic development in jazz improvisation.

To the experienced improviser, improvisation is largely a product of the memorization of standard jazz phrase patterns consciously and deliberately learned over a long period of time. When these patterns are employed in improvisation they usually appear in combined form—a portion of one phrase combined with a portion of another, and so on.

Example:

The most impressive jazz improvisers are frequently those who have built the largest vocabulary of jazz phrases (in all keys) and who have, through extensive experience, developed a keen feeling for when to employ and how to manipulate certain portions of their jazz vocabulary. However, an important area of jazz improvisation which is often overlooked is that of melodic reference--the manipulation of the melodic line. This is accomplished through the development of motives by employing such compositional techniques as repetition, sequence, variation and embellishment.

EDWARD B. Marks Music COMPANY / Exclusively Distributed By HAL•LEONARD® CORPORATION

Play and say the following intervals aloud:

Play a triad on each tone of the C Major scale:

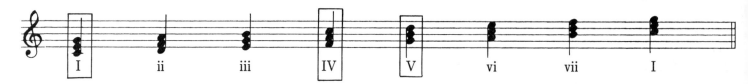

Basic blues structure uses only <u>three</u> of the above triads – the I, IV and V chords, usually in the following 12 bar arrangement:

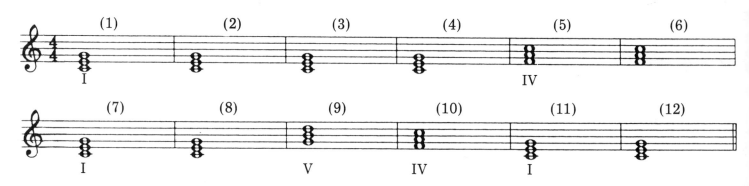

Play the following broken-chord melodic variation with the above chords:

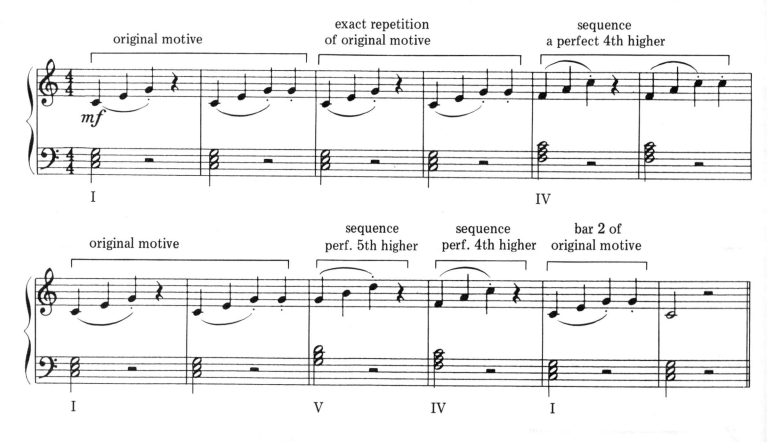

Note the two compositional (and improvisational) devices employed in the above melody—<u>exact repetition</u> and <u>sequence</u> (repetition of a motive on another scale degree.)

EXERCISES
Write and play sequences of the given motives at the indicated intervals:

Example:

ORIGIN OF THE BLUES

The 12 bar structure of the blues came about because the blues, when sung, contained three lines of poetry (the first two almost identical and the third a rhyming line) — each line of poetry using 4 bars of music.

Example: I feel so happy being here with you.
Oh I feel so happy being here with you.
And if you ever leave me, I'll be mighty blue.

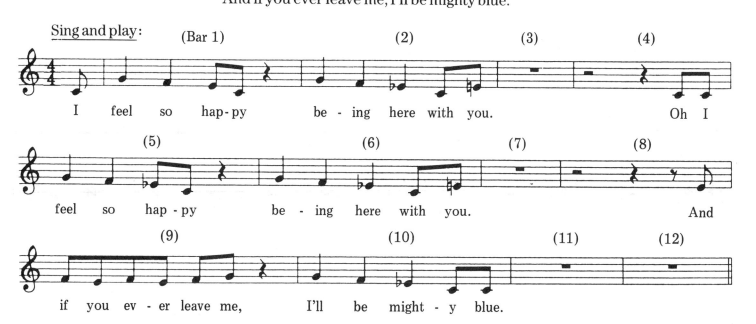

4

Play the following piano setting of the preceding blues:

I   IV   I   IV

I   V IV I
(anticipated)

* The substitute IV chord instead of the I chord is often employed in bar 2 of the blues by jazz musicians to create greater harmonic interest.

† The second phrase is a repetition of the first phrase, except for the alteration of E♮ (bar 1) to E♭ (bar 5) for a more consonant harmonization with the underlying chord.

In the following 12 bar blues, the composer states an original motive in bars 1–4 and then improvises the rest of the piece by using the devices of <u>sequence</u> and <u>repetition</u> of the original motive (or parts of it.)

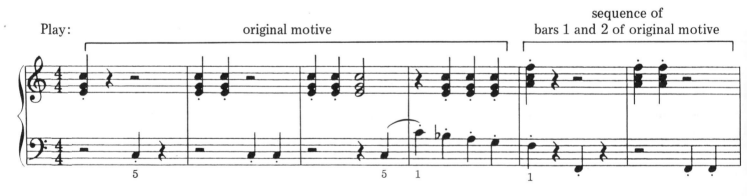

Play: original motive   sequence of
bars 1 and 2 of original motive

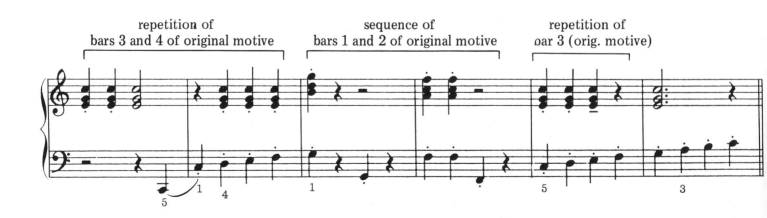

repetition of   sequence of   repetition of
bars 3 and 4 of original motive bars 1 and 2 of original motive bar 3 (orig. motive)

Note: Interpret all ♩♩ and ♩.♩ as ♩ ♪ in this book.

EXERCISES

Using <u>sequence</u> and <u>repetition</u>, improvise a 12 bar blues starting with the following 4 bar phrase:

Important suggestion: Tape and write down all improvisations for analysis purposes.

* The IV chord in bar 10 was intentionally avoided in order to make the use of sequence easier. Jazz musicians frequently make this V chord substitution in order to accomodate the melodic line, if necessary, or to create greater harmonic interest.

The realization of the above assignment appears on page 23.

Using <u>sequence</u> and <u>repetition</u>, improvise another 12 bar blues starting with the following 4 bar phrase:

The realization of the above assignment appears on page 23.

6

By playing chords on the tones of the G Major scale, we see that the I, IV and V chords (blues structure chords) in G Major are:

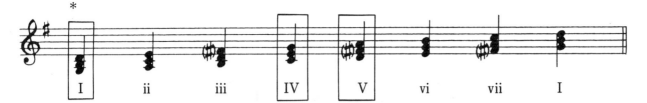

Using <u>repetition only</u>, improvise a 12 bar blues in G Major starting with the following 4 bar phrase:

* Any or all chords employed in blues structure may be changed to dominant 7th chords.

The author's realization of this assignment appears on page 24.

By playing chords on the tones of the F Major scale, we see that the I, IV and V chords in F Major are:

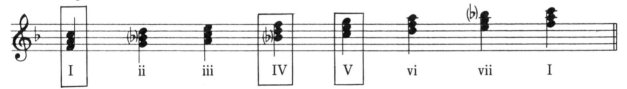

Using <u>repetition only</u>, improvise a 12 bar blues in F Major starting with the following 4 bar phrase: (Change any melodic tones where necessary to achieve a consonant harmony with the underlying chord.)

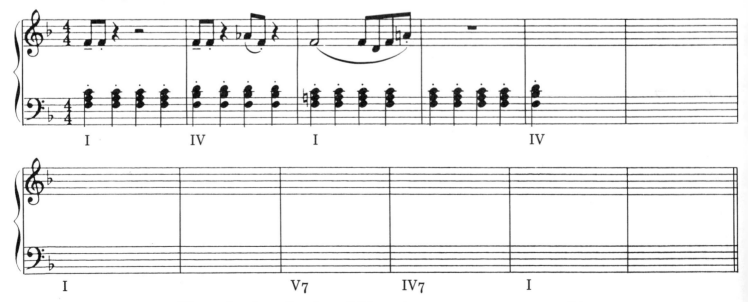

The author's realization of this assignment appears on page 24.

* Lower case Roman numerals identify minor and/or diminished triads.

By playing chords on the tones of the B♭ Major scale, we see that the I, IV and V chords in B♭ Major are:

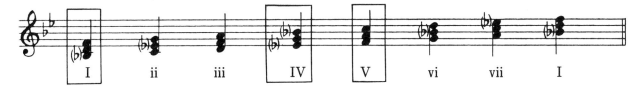

Using <u>sequence</u> and/or <u>repetition</u>, improvise a 12 bar blues in B♭ Major starting with the following 2 bar phrase:

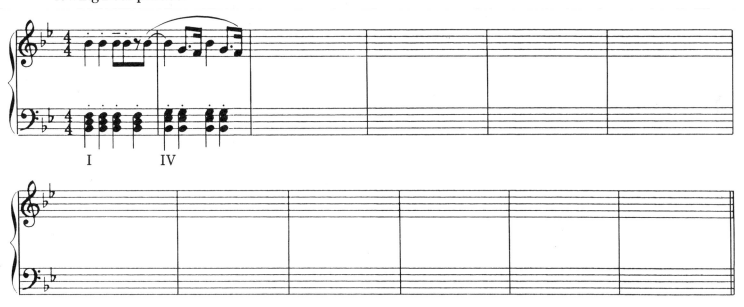

Now compose your own 2 or 4 bar motive in A♭ Major. Then complete the 12 bar blues by employing the improvisation techniques of <u>sequence</u> and/or <u>repetition</u>:

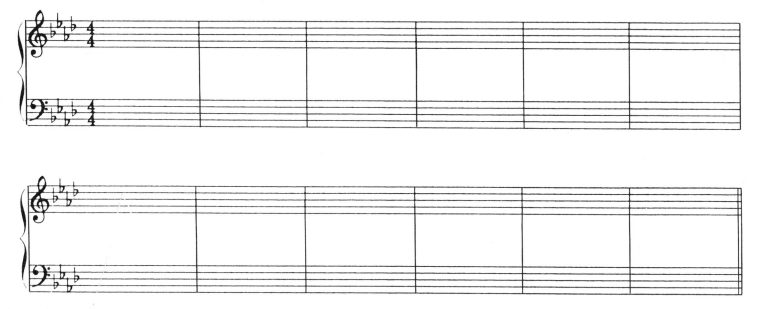

REPETITION AND SEQUENCE IN ALTERED FORMS

Sequence is not always accomplished as an exact repetition of a motive at another scale degree. Sequences may appear in <u>altered</u> forms such as:

<u>Rhythmic Diminution</u> – the melody remains unchanged, but note values become smaller.

<u>Intervallic Diminution</u> – the rhythm remains unchanged, but melodic intervals become smaller.

<u>Rhythmic Augmentation</u> – the melody remains unchanged, but note values become larger.

<u>Intervallic Augmentation</u> – the rhythm remains unchanged, but melodic intervals become larger.

<u>Fragmentation</u> – only a portion of a motive (rather than the entire motive) is treated in sequence or repetition.

<u>Complete Melodic Alteration</u> – the rhythm remains the same, but all pitch relationships change.

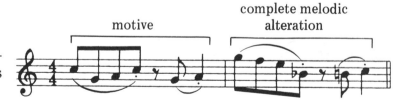

<u>Rhythmic Shift</u> – the melody and note values remain the same, but occur on different beats of the measure.

Retrograde – a motive presented backwards.

(Melodic) Inversion – a motive reflected upside down, all upward intervals mirrored in downward intervals of the same size, and vice versa.

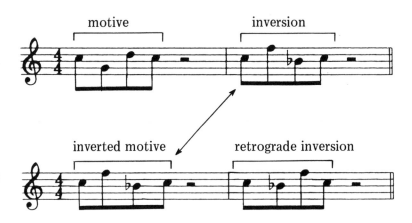

Retrograde Inversion – the inverted motive played backwards.

Chromatic Alteration – this device achieves a change of color without change of chord. (Blue notes– ♭3, ♭5, ♭7– are particularly effective chromatic alterations.)

Octave Displacement (Octave Shift) – a note or motive played an octave higher or lower in repetition or sequence.

The preceding alterations may be used in combination:

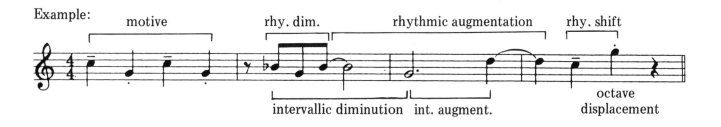

The following are two blues compositions. Play and study the various <u>altered forms</u> of repetition and <u>sequence</u> used here.

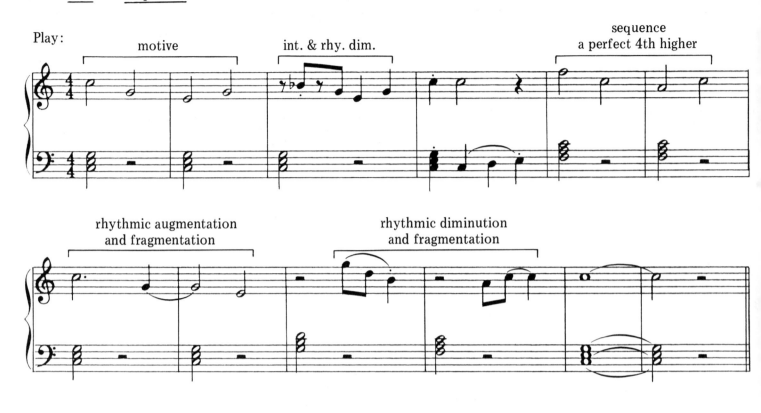

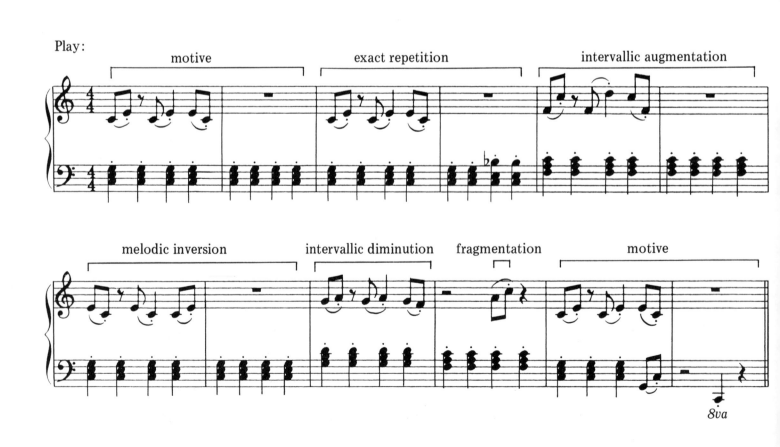

EXERCISES

Change each of the given motives as indicated:

Possible realizations of the above exercises appear on page 25.

Compose a 2 or 4 bar motive in G Major, and then improvise two choruses of the blues, employing exact repetition, sequence, and various altered forms of sequence (alone and/or in combination.)

Compose a 2 or 4 bar motive – this time in F Major – and then improvise two choruses of the blues, employing exact repetition, sequence, and various altered forms of sequence (alone and/or in combination.)

WEAK BEAT ORNAMENTS

<u>passing tone</u>*– a chromatic tone between two adjacent scale tones. (abbrev. P.T.)

<u>anticipation tone</u> – an anticipation tone between two adjacent scale tones. (abbrev. A.T.)

<u>échappée</u> – a tone occurring between two adjacent scale tones – the motion to the ornamenting tone being contrary to the motion between the scale tones. (abbrev. E.)

<u>cambiata</u> – a tone occurring between two adjacent scale tones – the motion to the ornamenting tone being the same as the motion between the scale tones. (abbrev. C.)

<u>neighbor tone</u> (upper or lower auxiliary tone) – a half or whole-step tone occurring between two of the same tones.(abbrev.N.T.)

STRONG OR WEAK BEAT ORNAMENT

<u>jazz appoggiatura</u>†– a leaping tone (leaping = interval larger than a 2nd) which then moves a major or minor 2nd in the opposite direction. (abbrev. J.A.)

OTHER ORNAMENTAL DEVICES

<u>grace note</u> – an ornamental tone whose time value is not counted in the rhythm. (abbrev. G.N.)

<u>repeated tone</u> – (abbrev. R.T.)

<u>tremolo</u> – the rapid alternation of two tones. (abbrev. trem.)

---

* In traditional usage, half or whole-step scale notes which, in a melody, pass between the tones of a triad or chord are sometimes referred to as passing tones. For the purpose of this book, however, these will be called <u>scale tones</u>; only half-step tones occurring between adjacent scale notes will be called <u>passing tones</u> in this volume.

† jazz appoggiatura - a <u>melodic</u> jazz embellishment that does not take into consideration the harmonic or rhythmic implications of the traditional appoggiatura.

scale tones – tones found in any scale other than the chromatic scale; chromatic scale tones would be heard as passing tones. (abbrev. S.T.)

chord tones – tones outlining any chord, including altered chords. (abbrev. C.T.)

free tone – an ornamental tone having no relationship to any chord being sounded. (abbrev. F.T.)

The following are examples of several different ways in which a given motive is embellished by the author: (Study the ornamental devices employed here.)

This grace note is a grace note fall-back – a half or whole-step grace note embellishing a tone which then "falls back" (descends) to the grace note tone.

An unlimited number of embellished versions of any given motive are possible.

EXERCISES

Add embellishment and ornamentation, <u>in two different treatments</u>, to each of the following passages wherever you feel the jazz flavor would be enhanced. (<u>All</u> the tones of each given passage <u>must</u> appear in the embellished versions for the purpose of these exercises.) Identify the devices employed.

Example:

The author's realizations of the above exercises appear on page 26.

The author's realizations of the above exercises appear on page 26.

The author's realizations of the above exercises appear on page 27.

The author's realizations of the above exercises appear on page 27.

20

20

21

The author's realizations of the above exercises appear on page 27.

Rewrite the improvisation you created on page 12, adding melodic embellishment and ornamentation (passing tones, neighbor tones, appoggiaturas, grace notes, etc.) to enhance the jazz flavor.

Rewrite the improvisation you created on page 13, adding melodic embellishment and ornamentation to enhance the jazz flavor.

APPENDIX
Author's Realizations

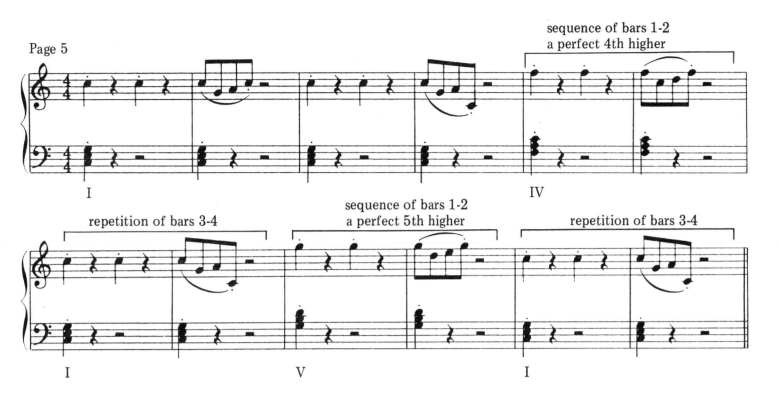

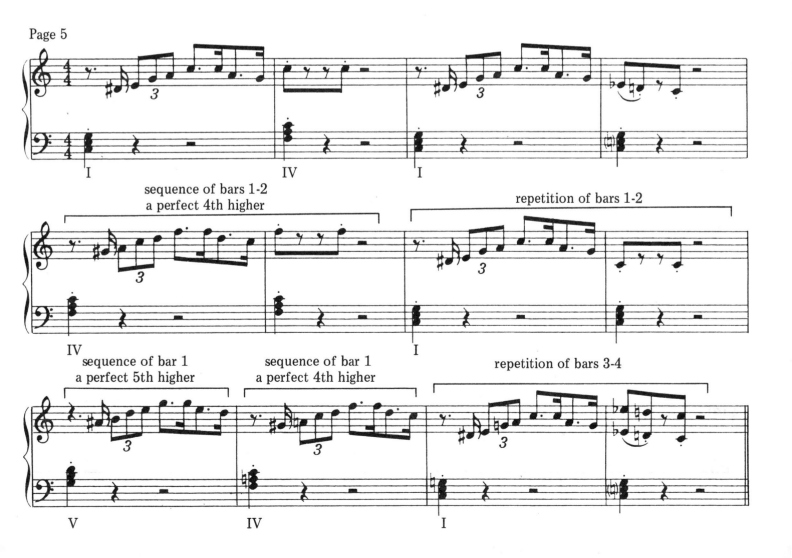

Author's Realizations

Page 6

Page 6

Author's Realizations

Page 16

Page 17

LEE EVANS JAZZ

METHOD BOOKS

BEGINNING JAZZ LEVEL

Easy Piano Jazz Rhythm Primer, The   00009037

INTERMEDIATE LEVEL

Beginning Jazz Improvisation   00009022
Starting with the basics, the student becomes actively involved in creating improvised melodies based upon blues progression, walking bass, boogie-woogie and other patterns.

The Elements Of Jazz   00009025
Covers syncopation, anticipation, blue notes, non-legato touch, 7th chords, walking bass, grace notes, ostinato (riffs), block chords, quartal jazz and other elements. Packed with solos utilizing these elements and techniques, plus four duets.

Further Experiences With The Elements Of Jazz   00009027
This volume carries forward in a very gradual manner jazz essentials for the early intermediate student, leading to improvisation.

Improvise By Learning How To Compose   00009054
This workbook teaches basic improvisational and compositional techniques, with particular emphasis on melodic development in jazz.

Jazz Keyboard Harmony   00009036
The definitive, comprehensive chord workbook in jazz improvisation. Covers chord substitution, voice leading, interpretation of chord symbols. Complete theoretical information. Brings improvising ability to all pianists.

Learning To Improvise Jazz Accompaniments   00009041
Devoted to the development of improvisational skills in the jazz idiom. Explains the functions and creation of accompaniments to give melodic lines. Gives the pianist a comfortable feeling for improvising.

INTERMEDIATE/UPPER INTERMEDIATE LEVEL

**The Jazz Tetrachord Approach To Keyboard Jazz
  Improvisation**   00009039
A workbook which utilizes selected jazz tones and a wide variety of rhythmic patterns in a manner that makes the student's jazz expressions sound authentic.

UPPER INTERMEDIATE/ADVANCED LEVEL

Modes And Their Use In Jazz   00009043
This unique book provides pianists (and all instrumentalists) with a comprehensive view of diatonic modes — Ionian, Dorian, Phrygian, Lydian, Mixolydian, Aeolian, Locrian — the way they may be identified in all keys, developing a working knowledge in non-jazz and jazz contexts. Complete jazz pieces in the various modes. Many modal exercises.

TECHNIQUE

EASY JAZZ LEVEL

Easy Jazz With I-IV-V & Their 7th Chords   00009049
Easy-to-play, authentically jazzy harmonization by Lee Evans of originals and standards, using I-IV-V and their 7th chords. Chord exercises. Several major and minor keys employed.

INTERMEDIATE LEVEL

Jazz-Flavored Sequential Patterns & Passages   00009034
The employment of sequences for finger dexterity, and as a compositional technique. Short jazz pieces in every major and minor key.

Jazz-Flavored Broken Triads   00009032
Total training in fingering patterns for broken triads in all major and minor keys. Unusually excellent jazz rhythm training. Includes pertinent short jazz etudes.

Jazz-Flavored Scale Patterns & Exercises   00009033
All major, melodic minor and harmonic minor scales are presented in a jazz framework, utilizing an extraordinary range of jazz rhythms.

The Rhythms Of Jazz   00009046
Complete, original piano repertoire materials illustrating virtually all types of categories of jazz rhythms.

REPERTOIRE

EASY JAZZ LEVEL

Jack & Jill Jazz   00009030
Brings the feeling of jazz to children's songs and nursery rhymes — beginning rhythms and chords for the pianist starting jazz.

More Jack & Jill Jazz   00009044
Early intermediate arrangements of more children's songs for enjoyment in building easy repertoire.

One Finger Piano   00009051
Solo piano piece.

Jazz Interpretations Of Popular American Folk Songs   00009035
A number of well-known folk songs adapted with an authentic jazz flavor.

EARLY INTERMEDIATE LEVEL

Easy Jazz Christmas Duets   00009024
Lee's first duet book by demand — simple yet tasteful arrangements for four hands-one piano of the popular arrangements from his solo piano books. **Jazz Up Your Christmas** and **Christmas—Modern Piano Impressions**.

Introduction To 16th Notes Book 1   00009028
Introduces 16th notes in the context of time signatures having 4 as the bottom number.

A Musical Christmas For Easy Piano   00009045
14 Christmas classics — plays easy but sounds musical! When was the last time you saw that winning combination in a solo piano Christmas album?

INTERMEDIATE LEVEL

Amazing Grace   00009052
Solo piano piece.

Christmas—Modern Piano Impressions   00009023
Follows the popular earlier **Jazz Up Your Christmas** folio with eleven more distinctively arranged Christmas Carols.

Famous Irish Airs   00009026
New modern impressions of 11 Irish melodies with the sound of a professional performing pianist yet only intermediate difficulty.

God Bless' The Child   00009053
Solo.

Jazz Suite For Piano   00009038
Solo.

Jazz Up Your Christmas   00009040
12 Christmas carols in fresh perspective. Excellent arrangements in good taste, the full contents may be played as a concert suite.

Malaguena   00009042
Simplified duet - 1 piano, 4 hands.

More (Mondo Cane)   00009055
Solo.

Rock Styles For Piano   00009047
Gives the pianist a history of rock styles from the 50's — from the simple to the complex. Original compositions illustrating each rock expression. Early rock 'n' roll, rhythm 'n' blues, country, pop rock, etc.

Watercolors   00009050
Solo.

Travel The Keyboard Jazz Highway   00009048
Supplementary jazz pieces at the early intermediate level, each featuring a musical point — "Rest Area" uses rests in music, "Detours Ahead" deals with modulations, "Two Way Street" and "Divided Highway" are duets, naturally, etc.

Wonderful! Wonderful!   00009056
Solo.

INTERMEDIATE/UPPER INTERMEDIATE LEVEL

Advanced Rock Styles For Piano   00009021
Continues the expansion of rock styles and greater development — Motown, Southern, funk, disco, dixieland, jazz-rock, etc.

UPPER INTERMEDIATE/ADVANCED LEVEL

Famous Jazz Piano Styles   00009057
Original song arrangements by Lee Evans highlighting the stylistic character of eight of history's greatest jazz pianists. Includes a recording of each composition performed by Evans.

ADVANCED LEVEL

Introduction & Toccata In Jazz   00009058
Solo.